POETRY
TO LIVE BY

KARON SCHLICKER

WESTBOW
PRESS®
A DIVISION OF THOMAS NELSON
& ZONDERVAN

WestBow Press books may be ordered through booksellers or by contacting:

WestBow Press
A Division of Thomas Nelson & Zondervan
1663 Liberty Drive
Bloomington, IN 47403
www.westbowpress.com
1 (866) 928-1240

ISBN: 978-1-9736-3319-8 (sc)
ISBN: 978-1-9736-3320-4 (e)

Library of Congress Control Number: 2018907895

Print information available on the last page.

WestBow Press rev. date: 12/11/2018

FOREWORD

I was never very good at writing poetry. I would have those assignments in school to write a poem about something and I never knew exactly how to fix it. Whatever I had written certainly was not poetry!!

Poetry-it can evoke many emotions and thoughts from the author as well as the hearer. God can use poetry in our lives to convict and to bring glory to Himself. I have the privilege of knowing this particular poet and I know that her desire is to bring the reader closer to God.

Karon has been writing poetry for many years. She has written poems daily for the 15 or so years that I have know her. She shares them with the congregation on a regular basis. It is because of the encouragement of one her dearest friends that she is publishing these for others to enjoy.

The ability that she has to put words on paper is truly a gift from God and Karon would be the first to tell you that He is the One to get the glory. I would like to say thank you, Karon, for sharing your gift with the rest of us. Her wish, and mine, is that you are able to focus on the Creator as you read these wonderful poems. God bless you.

Laura Grenier
Secretary First Baptist Church
Of Moses Lake, Washington

PREFACE

I was encouraged by my Bible Study Group to publish the poetry I have been sharing with them for spiritual growth and encouragement.

Introduction

These poems are written by the inspiration of God for spiritual growth, and encouragement. It is life in poetry form.

CONTENTS

SERVE HIM

I'll serve Him no matter the cost
To draw all who are like I was—lost,

To do all he assigns me to do,
Never doubting Him anew,

Always trusting He knows best,
Better—much better—than the rest.

For He is our one true God,
Even if we are not willing to applaud.

I will not deny my Creator
Nor His Son, who has made me greater—

Greater than I could ever be on my own,
Made soft and pliable this heart of stone.

So how can I count the cost of what He's done,
This God man—God's own Son?

ANOTHER STRIPE
ON HIS BACK

Every time I fall, I put another thorn in the crown on His head,
And I wish that I had it on instead.

Every time I disobey, I put another stripe on His back
Just because of the will I lack.

Every time I deny Him, I nail Him to the cross,
And it pushes me farther away from Him, and I feel deeply the loss.

So every time I do these things, I try to keep in mind
A very great love He has for me I find.

It makes it that much easier to not do them again
To know the agony I put Him through, the very great pain.

FOUNDATIONAL STONE

It starts today; Jesus is going home,
Our Savior and foundational stone.

But before He goes, He has work to do.
The benefits are for me and you.

It's not easy, this work that must be done,
And He's the only qualified one.

Now on His shoulders, He must bear the cross
So that our very souls won't be lost.

Then He'll go home, but in His place,
He'll send the Holy Spirit of grace

To guide us, help us, and call us home
With the knowledge we won't be alone.

An eternity is what we will spend with Him,
Singing praises and glory then.

A Day unto God

When we go into His house to worship Him, do we?
Or do we go in to just gossip with each other?

When we sing our praises, are they to Him? Are they?
Or are they just to fill the silence and put on a show?

When we are in the services, do we go there to learn? Do we?
Or do we go there and let our minds wander
Or just to show we are there?
When we go to church on Sunday, are we
on our best behavior? Are we?

Or are we two different people, the one we show
to Christians and the one we show to
The world?
Do we love our God wholly without blemish or shame?
Do we? Or do we only care on the one day we share?

WHY MY FACE IS TURNED UP

Why is my face turned up to the sky?
Because I feel I can't get any lower, no matter how hard I try.

Why are my eyes closed? Of light there is not a trace
Because I want to see Your wonderful face.

Lord, You know my every part,
And You know what lies deep in my heart.

So on me Your blessings lay,
And know that I love You; humbly I pray

That I want to get to know You better
Without any chains, binds, or fetters.

That I might know You as You know me,
With You eternally I'll always be.

WHERE ARE THE TEARS?

Where are the tears that should be
Cried for His people?

Where are the tears for our sin?
Where are the tears for all the evil?

Where are the tears for the people of hopelessness?
Where are the tears for the degradation of the Christian?

Where are the tears for the people's callousness?
Where are the tears for human's overall plan?

Where are the tears? O Lord, where are the tears?
Are You the only one who cries for humans?
Who fears?

Not Worth It

Christ died for me, and I was not worth it.
I didn't believe in Him—lazy and didn't do my bit.

I doubt my closest friend would do that.
But Jesus did; He went down that path.

How can I repay a debt that cannot be redeemed?
It just cannot be done, no matter how I planned or schemed.

But there are some things I can do;
One is confessing Him to you.

The other is living how He wants me to live
And to give how He wants me to give.

Another is to put my whole trust in Him
Above that of the world and its sin.

So I pledge today my live to give to You.
Then I'll sit back and watch the wonders You do.

ALL THE TEARS
ARE THE SAME

All the tears are the same,
No matter what their name.
No matter what side you're on.
The people you love are still gone.
War is a very evil pride

Where even innocent babies die.
Where is God's love in the hearts of these men
Who decide their neighbors need to be condemned?
How can they justify and watch the horror thereof,
The brutality and hardened hearts from love?

How can they do this awful thing of sin
Just because they're different from without and within?
How can they justify to God their disobedience
By not loving their neighbor as themselves in compliance?

I pray to God to put His love in their hearts
And nevermore from God depart.
So come join me now for them to pray,
And by joining together His love to stay.

THE ROBBERY OF OUR FREEDOM

Your child is walking down the street,
And upon her back a red jacket that really looks neat.

But not far away, tragedy awaits
For a gang of blue coats lying along the way.

Then they are upon her, and her throat they do slash,
And happy and triumphant, away they do dash.

Another child is down and lost
Because of gang rivalry; they don't count the cost.

And just because of ignorance and not knowing about
The bright red jacket of the rival gang it would definitely shout.

And the freedoms of our children and their
clothing are lost in the mire
Of gangland rivalry because an excuse they don't require.

Just the knowledge the jacket or hat is the right color—
That's reason enough to eliminate the other.

We must do something, people, not just sit on our laurels.
For those children, dear God, don't have any morals.

We didn't think it would come to our small town.
But it's here, people; just ask the kids—they'll
tell you; they'll tell you it's around.

We must do something about it, or we'll soon be a like LA.
Then, my friend, it will be no holiday.

Some come together as friends, in prayer groups, and alone;
We must come against this thing, these hearts that are stone.

We must come against this thing right from the start,
Or we will find, if we don't, it will break every mother's heart.

Silent Scream

It won't be long, and I will be born, and I'm not sure she wants me.
But the time will come. It is God's plan, and that's as it should be.

I will see all the beauty and the glory of the world.
All the joy and love in me will be unfurled.

To see what importance I am to God's plan,
To be weak or strong and where I stand.

But all this now is but a dream
As I cry and silently scream.

They are taking my life—my being from me.
Now none of that can happen, can ever be.

FORGIVEN

There are many things in life that we find hard to forgive ourselves—
Deep, dark things that we don't want anyone to delve.

So we think that if we can't, how can our God?
But then I remember the murderer on the
cross; God did not think that odd.

We must remember His mercy and grace.
He sent His Son so of our sins there would be no trace.

All we have to do is have deep, repentant hearts,
Give them to Him so that He can start

To show us not only to forgive ourselves in time,
But also to forgive others and let His light shine.

Therefore, we are forgiven when we accept this—
Not only that, but we are totally His.

LOVE ENOUGH

He's loving enough to love even me,
Even though it's the real me.

He forgives all my iniquity
And works at changing me to what I should be.

He will not leave me alone in my sin
Because He wants in me a new life to begin.

He molds me and makes me to the shape He wants
For His glory, praise, and love to vaunt.

He wraps me and cradles me in His loving cocoon,
Surrounding me with His strength morning, night, and noon.

He fills me so with His love and grace
That of the old me, there is no trace.

Such a mighty and awesome God He is;
I want everyone I know to be His.

THE TEACHER

The teacher has a tremendous responsibility
To teach children God's Word (the reality),

To open their minds and hearts to His love
With prayers and guidance from above.

To mend and mold is what they do.
They need the help you can give them too.

Your work and mine are what they need.
So, won't you help them? This I plead!

If we want strong children in Christ,
Don't you think it's worth the price?

JOSEPH—ASSIGNMENT FROM GOD

Joseph, a very gentle man,
Loving and giving as is God's command.

Loving Mary, not wanting her shames,
Not willing that she be defamed

Even though he hurt deep within
At Mary's pregnancy before their life together began.

He anguished over what to decide
But was willing to set her quietly aside.

Then the angel came and consoled his heart,
And the birth of God's Son was Mary's part.

The burden he had of caring and raising Him as his own,
Training Him as the Lord would condone.

How can we understand the essence of the man
That shows us how to in God's stead stand?

And to think—it's his very own Savior.
May we be like him in our behavior.

PLUGGED INTO CHRIST

So you say you're a Christian?
So you say you belong to the Son of Man?
You say your weighed down with troubles?
Don't you know the work you'll just cobble?
Why are you not electrified by the Spirit?
Why do you not want to hear it?
Why have you not taken hold?
Don't you know He carries the load?
Don't you know you should be plugged into Christ?
Don't you know He'll help you fight?
Don't you understand He can help you?
Don't you know what to do?
Don't you understand He is the Power?
And upon you all His love He has showered?
Don't you grasp you just call on His Name?
That this is not a game?
Don't you know you just have to ask?
And you can just sit ack and in His love bask?
Are you plugged into Christ?
Don't you know that you have that right?
He who has sacrificed all,
If you hang on, He wont' let you slip and fall.

Self-Will

Isn't self will a marvelous thing.
It comes even before the King of Kings.

It's great to know your always right,
No matter the cost, no matter the plight.

To know that you've earned it that's plain
Well its simply all that You've gained.

And isn't it marvelous to see you've done so well,
Even though self will has sent you to Hell.

A Gift Received a gift Returned

I have searched and searched for a gift to give Jesus.
I've looked high and low and didn't know where to find it.
What do you give the Omnipotence, Immanuel (God with us)?
Slowly but surely it came to me, little by little, bit by bit.

You can't wrap it and put it under a tree.
You can't see it or touch it or even smell it.
But the gift of love you can give to be like a candle
Glowing and wondrously lit.
Obeying, serving, and a washer of feet.

Loving one another with a freedom of heart.
But it is still not enough, we must give Him lost souls.
So I will try with great zeal to so my part.
To give all these things to you will be my goal.

For this very precious gift Jesus gave to me,
Now as a gift to Him I pass it along to you.
Not greater gift can there for Him be
Than knowing this I have done and will continue to do.

IT'S NOT ABOUT ME

I work hard in the worship team
And in Sunday School word of life glean.

I sometimes work in the nursery and toddlers
And give encouragement to mothers and fathers.

Sometimes I make the Sunday morning coffee
And send cards for Birthdays, Anniversaries, and Sympathy.

Outside my church I try to walk a straight and narrow pathway.
And care for my family and friends God's way.

All these things I do for His Glorification.
For it's not about me, but because to Him I owe my salvation.

Holding On

My God, Lord and Savior. I'm holding on to Your hand tightly,
As through these very dark days I stumble down unknown roads.

I do not take the lessons I'm learning lightly.
Knowing that Your helping me carry my load.

Everyone asks how I do it and marvel at the strength.
I tell them lord, it is not mine but they still insist it is.

But if they have any thought at length,
They would understand it is not I doing this.

It is for Your glory, Your honor, it is only You.
May they see it Lord, and comprehend.

That everything I try to say, everything I try to do,
Is only ever Your command.

THEN THERE WAS YOU

I was wandering around in a lost world.
Searching and searching for I knew not what.
Looking for someone who didn't with me get bored.
Or who cared enough for me the doors they didn't shut.

Then there was You!

Someone who is with me when I was down.
Someone who is there when I cried aloud.
I looked here and there and all around.
You were just waiting for me not to be so proud.

Then there was You.

So come what may I knew what I had to do,
Get down on my knees and pray for forgiveness.
To give my life wholly and totally to You.
Now my life is new because of Your mercifulness.

Then there was You!

Because I've accepted Jesus in His righteousness,
I now have eternal life.
Because of His loving kindness,
And His sacrifice beyond price.

Now there is always ever You!

When I First Discovered You, O God

My feet was froze instantly, one shoe was lost immediately.
I didn't know when I lost the other, the feeling was gone totally.
We walked on a car and had to dig to fined if anyone was there,
That no one was in it was a great relief, was our greatest care.
I was getting tired by then, and the only way
we could see where we were going,
Was the telephone poles all in a row, because
of the snow that was blowing.
We passed an animal shed and I wanted to
stop by my husband knew, you see,
That I would die before he could come back to me.

I knew by then I was in serious trouble and I needed help real fast.
I called on the Lord and told Him if He saved my life He
could take my legs if He just gave me the strength to last.
It wasn't for me that I made that plea.
I didn't want my husband to feel guilt
because of what happened to me.
Well the Lord got me through and with flying colors too.
But the doctors didn't understand it, they thought
they would have to amputate a toe times two.
God gave me more than one gift that very special day.
For with His life my debt He had already paid.
He gave the gift of love and understanding,
oh, but more, much more than this.
He gave me life eternal, and greeted me with an Holy Kiss.

WE KNOW THE REST OF THE STORY

As we look around us fear could easily take over
And have us rushing to shelter for cover.

But we know the rest of the Story.
About how the Son will come in all His glory.

We know that it didn't just end with His birth,
When God came down to earth.

We know it continued to the cross
To relieve us from all the dross.

And on that liberating day
When He rose form the grave.

With a promise to come back again
To take us home His adopted kin.

So on this His Birthday we always pray,
Hurry, Lord Jesus, come back our way.

A NEW PEW

The first pew is always empty.
Why do you think that is so?

The preacher is closer and advantages are many.
Don't you think that's better? No?

Are you afraid of the attention he might pay
Or he might catch you napping?

Or course, if you are there he might be the first for you to pray.
Then there is the word he teaches. To You he is calling.

So if you get a chance sit in the first pew.
See what a difference it makes.
To have an out look that's brand new.
For your life is at stake.

LEFT TO THEMSELVES

There are those of whom are hard to please.
And think you can do everything they can with ease.

There are those who only wish to control.
And your very lives in their hands hold.

There are those who only wish to hide away.
And from trials and tribulations stay.

There are those who only wish to please man,
And in that regard do everything they can.

But they don't know that wasn't what God intended.
And furthermore they don't wish to delve,
Instead in the end, they are only left to themselves.

The World and Sometimes Us

Why should I care the condition of her state?
Why should I care whether she's at heavens gate.

It's not my problem man.
Let someone else help if they can.

She's not by business, not my life.
She's not my sister, mother, wife.

I'm not responsible for her care.
Not my load to share.

Let her family or friends take the risk.
She's someone else's problem, that's what she is.

That's the outlook as the world sees'
Or may be it's only just me!

No Decision

No decision is a no decision.
Sitting on the fence doesn't work at all.

So, you'd better understand your position,
If your not totally His, then down you fall.

There is no half ways or maybes
Or making you mind up at the last minuet.

You know Jesus already paid the price, He made it easy.
So why is it so hard to make your choice, yet,

I could see if your life was better without Him.
I could see it if what you gave up was good.

But it's worse living in a life of sin.
Living in Him would be better, that should be understood.

The only thing I can do for you
Is uplift you in fervent prayer.

That is the best thing in can do.
Is to leave you in His gentle care.

THE REASON

In heaven the angles singing, a glorious sound.
Trumpets calling through the earth all around.

A star shining brightly in the east.
Announcing the birth of the Holy Child from the least.

To bring redemption unto all the earthly men,
After the life teachings end.

Always remembering the beginning but never forgetting the cross.
He's done everything in His power to have no one lost.

Now, it's time to do our part answering His call,
To miss this great opportunity would be worst of all.

It would be a shame if for you He lived His life in vain.
Don't be the one left behind when He comes again.

OWN THING

Are you doing your own thing?
All the while in trouble and complaining?

Are you waling down the crooked path,
Flirting with God's wrath?

Are you pushing your limitations,
Knowing that there is a break down in calculations?

Are you no relying on the Lord,
Being of one accord?

When are you going to learn,
When are you going to discern,

That the only life you need
Is in Jesus to be freed?

Is He your King

Is He your king or is He your King?
Exactly where do you put Him in your life?

Do you bring Him everything
Or do you only come to Him in strife?

Do you acknowledge him as your Savior and nothing more?
Or do you have a breaking heart when you don't give Him your
all? For you, do you know exactly what He has in store,
Or do you ignore and therefore fall? Are you
blasé' about the Lord as if He is afar?

Or are you overwhelmed by His closeness and His abiding love?
Are you wishing upon a star? Or are you depending
on your Master and King from above?

Anything He Wants

He can do anything He wants to,
After all, He is the creator.

Who are we to demand it our way in things we do?
It only causes pain and torture.

We fight hard to get our own way, only to find
out we've hindered ourselves in the fray.

If only we'd listen when He talks
And not run when He wants us to walk.

Then we could bring glory to His Name
As we spread throughout the world His fame.

MAKING SURE

Do we live as though we believe God and not just mouth the words?
Are we living the lifestyle of Jesus or in it does he world merge?

Is our light shining bright or visibly very dim?
Can we save the drowning man or do we let
Him sink because we can't swim?

How many times has the world seen your life
And never guessed you are Christ's wife.

Everything we say and do come under the scrutiny of the world.
So, lets make sure that what the world sees isn't
cheap stones but very precious pearls.

CHRISTMAS' TRUE MEANING

Thinking of Christmas and all it means,
Not presents or food, trees, no not any of these things.

Not lights or decorations on the windows,
Not cold wintry snows.

But the life of the little baby born for a purpose,
That if we rely on Him and in Him put our trust,

That or very souls depend upon what we choose.
If Jesus we win, if the world we lose.

So, humbly I pray, keep me in the right pathway
That I might not ever decide to stray.

That I work wholly for the Lord
And confess the Word, which in me You've stored.

That everyone might enjoy Christmas night
And make a small change in the world and it's plight.

WE SHOUL BE DIFFERENT

We should be different, but we are so weak.
So afraid, mild and meek.

God give us everything we need,
But, don't send me is what I plead.

Fear and laziness abounds in our soul.
Instead of love, compassion, that should be our goal.

But we will have to answer to Him if we don't change our ways.
In the day we come to Him face to face.

So, we'd better be pleading with Him to help change our lives,
Or we'll have no jewels in our crown in our eternal life.

WITHOUT EXCUSE

We're without excuse for there is testimony all around.
We must open up our eyes and hearts, for it does abound.

It's in the air we breath.
It's in the abundance of trees.

It's in the birds in the air.
And in the desert bare.

It's in the stars in the sky
And in the mountains high.

But more than what we can see or feel,
It's His Spirit inside to all be revealed.

Therefore, we are without excuse,
You can either take the cross or refuse.

WHY DO YOU SERVE HIM

Why do you serve? What is the motive of your heart?
Is it a real love for God or is it just for man's part?

You must be jealous of the reason,
That you are only God's person.

For only then will you gain crowns
And avoid a critical frown.

Besides, when done right, the blessings of God are great
And the results of the service of which He did create.

Giving Him all the fame and glory
For the one true God, jus and holy.

You were not There

You were not there – on the cross.
Feeling the crown of thorns upon His head.

Nor the stones upon His back they tossed,
Nor the stripes filled with sharp things embedded.

Nor the jeers and sneers as He passed by.
Not the sins that were dumped on His very soul.

Not the despair as His father turned away His head, He cried.
And felt deep rejection as He hung on the pole.

Nor going down to the pit of Hell,
All covered in death and sin.

But in the third day He defeated it with a yell
And for the world arose again.

OF TWO MINDS

Do you know of which direction you find Christ?
Do you keep changing your mind and are doubtful?

Do you think He's your all in all or a thoughts that's nice?
Listening to anyone but the Holy Spirit will be unhelpful.

God says being of two minds or double minded isn't believing at all
And that He has no time for people such as that.

So, repent and trust in Him before you eternally fall.
That you might be where Jesus the Son is at.

A Babe

One more babe born, one more of the many poor.
What would make this one special, this one
they would try to make into lore?

Why would angels sing to shepherds? Why would wise
men come to worship Him? Why would so many try
To kill Him and ruin His reputation when matured? Why
is it when we see the cross we are so very Enamored?

The answer is found in the Word of God, in love story so sweet,
One of God's special promises, one of His special treats.

You can find it in Luke and even Matthew too.
You can find it in the old prophesies made to me and you.

So, remember when celebrating this Christmas,
it should be observed all year round.
No greater way can we try to repay than that, I have found.

BE THANKFUL

Be ye thankful for every little thing.
Give glory to God, His praises to sing.

Be ye thankful for the flowers that grow
And even the weeds that He does bestow.

For without the weeds we wouldn't appreciate the roses.
Without the thorns we wouldn't appreciate what He blesses.

Give glory to God for every thought you have had
And giving them to Him makes Him glad.

By giving Him our weaknesses He gives His strength
And helping us with our problems at length.

Hold on to His hand through thick and thin.
There is no better place to begin.

JUST ANOTHER GOD

Are your treating God as just another god on the list?
Or are you loving Him as He insists?

Do you use Him as a personal gift giver,
When in fact He should be the receiver?

Why do we never put God high enough
And just use Him for personal stuff?

He is our Creator and maker of all things.
Why are we not letting this our heart sing?

Why can't we let Him be top most—God,
And Him our hands and lips applaud?

BAD HEART

"What is you heart condition?" asks the man of God.
Is it full of fat? Are your arteries diseased or clogged?

Is if filled with all kinds of stuff you shouldn't eat?
Are your veins clogged with junk clear down to your feet?

How glad to know there is a cleansing way.
Although not painless it's safe and no price to pay.

The doctor is Jesus, faithful and true.
No other One will ever do.

DON'T

If it's the worry path your taking, Don't.
If it's anger that your allowing to take over. Don't.

If it's the cares of this world your running after. Don't.
If you think it's only by your ability. Don't

If your letting prejudices grow in your heart. Don't.
If your letting a me attitude take over. Don't

If your ignoring God's wisdom. Don't.
If your allowing Satan to rule your heart. Don't.

When I can no Longer See

I hope I have memorized Your Word,
That it may be hidden deep inside of me.
The precious word of You, Lord,
More than life is what I need.

When I can no longer see and need to hear.
Help me to recall all I've learned.
Recall all the love from You That's near
What inside me you have burned.

Bring to mind all the times we have shared together,
Putting me through the darkened night.
Knowing You were there my precious Savior,
Making even the dark paths bright.

But if that time shall never be,
As I read great enjoyment I will get.
And Your word will burn inside of me,
That shows the brilliance of You, and I am humbled that we met.

A Birthday Gift

What can I give Him poor as I am?
If I were a shepherd I would give Him a lamb.

If I were a wise man I would do my part.
I would find out what to do right from the start.

If I were a rich man it would be harder to do,
But then, he would help me give it to you.

If I were a humble man I would give Him my weakness,
That He might make me strong to show His gracefulness.

Yet, what can I give Him who has nothing to worth of which to part?
I can only give Him my heart?

Is This In Me

You wonder when you see the attitudes that come out in people,
Is the ugliness of this in my soul full?

We don't see ourselves through other people's yes.
We sometimes don't see their response or hear their cries.

When we do we wonder is that really in me?
How could we let it be?

That is what the sacrifice of Your Son is all about?
So give Him a Hallelujah shout.

I thank You that You bring these things to our attention.
That we can give them back to You with no hesitation.

That You change us to make them right.
And that You fill us with Your Holy Light.

Greed, Fear, Insecure

My life is full of greed, although I try to brush it away.
It always seems to creep in, it is hard to hold at bay.

It's also full of fear of things I can't control
And before I know it my peace has been stole.

Then there is the insecurity of always living like that
And I can get lost in it not knowing where I'm at.

But there is an answer to all the problems that plague.
It's really very clear not at all vague.

The answer of course, is Jesus just call
His name and He'll answer you.

You can't ask for a better solution
As these problems He sees you through.

THE LAW

The Law is to love God! Do I really do that in my heart?
It is his first great command so am I doing my part?

Is the words I profess real?
Do I from Him some of my heart steal?

When I say I truly love Him,
Do I mean it deep down within?

I'm not proving it by what I say and do.
Are you the same way too?

I try real hard and I want it to be
Real deep down in the heart of me.

The one thing I can rely on, His promises or me and you.
They really do come true.

That's one of His promises. He'll be with me forever.
I want always to love Him for He'll leave me Never.

Thank You Note To God

Dear God, I'm sending you this note
To let you know that to You my life I will devote.

Knowing full well that the best is yet to be.
When at last I will meet you just beyond the Crystal Sea.

That a grain of sand a pearl will one day make
And like me, to perfect, a lot of work it will take.

But still to be a pearl beyond price
I will humbly work and take Your advice.

This not is to let your know that I'll commit myself to Christ the Lord.
No other possibly do and to do otherwise I can't afford.

So I'm saying praise and thanks for all the work You've done,
Hallelujah and Glory to God, in the name of Your dear Son.
From Your loving daughter, with humbleness,
Who, in You puts her complete trust.

REMINDER OF CHRISTMAS

This is a reminder of what is Christmas Day.
And of the crucifixion later.

Of our debt the baby was to pay.
And our blessings in the facts of the matter.

So hear the bells that are rung,
The gifts that are given.

That there are special songs to be sung
For the one that has truly risen.

So on this special day
Remember His whole life was for a purpose.

That by His side we would chose to stay
And that all was done for us.

AND HE PRAYED FOR ME

He loved me so much He prayed for me,
This little bit of nothing and never could be.
But He cried out in longing and love
to His Father above.

He asked Him to keep me, love me and send the spirit to guide me.
It fills me with awe that one such as He could
pray for me on bended knee.

He prayed for me with all His gloriousness, Power and might.
So that I might make it through the darkest of night.

How mighty is our Jesus, Savior and Friend.
How satisfyingly beautiful that He is with me to the end.

My Shadow

On the days I need a boost it makes me look a beauty.
On the days I need humbled, it makes me a fright.
For I look and it is there no matter where I go. It is with
me in the morning and it is with me in the night.
It is someone I can talk to and it don't talk back.
It is never over critical in pointing out what I lack.

It is always ever there to take the loneliness away.
It is always close beside me, I know it's there to stay.

I'm not speaking of the grayness of which of me it is a part.
But am speaking of dear Jesus who lives within my heart.

So thank You dear Jesus, who is ever always there.
I put myself totally and completely in Your care.

Till the darkness in me becomes light and I'm with You on that shore.
I will always be with you for ever and ever more.

STEPPING STONE OR STUMBLING BLOCK

The actions I take, which way will they go?
Will they be a good example or just for show?

The things that I do, are they stepping stones,
Or are the for me alone?

The things people see, are they stumbling blocks?
Will they be in for a shock?

So I ask You, Lord, help me be a stepping stone not a stumbling block.
That someone might not come upon a gate that's locked.

That they may find Your door wide open,
Because they see in me Jesus the son.

CHRIST EMBEDDED

The biggest thing against a Christian is self.
To work everything out for you wealth.

Cursing when things don't exactly go right
And letting everyone feel the power of your might.

Being a poor witness for Jesus the Son
And not relying on the Holy One.

All these things are to His discredit
Making us in the end regret it.

So I pray for all, me included
That we get self out and have Christ embedded.

CANNOT UNDERSTAND

I cannot understand why the Lord would choose me,
A cracked and flawed vessel?

To bring His word and make them see,
Thy marvelous works with which they wrestle?

To help open their eyes and hearts,
About all thy love You wish to impart.

Why You've chosen me I cannot comprehend,
When I look around there are much better men.

Since I can't understand why,
I'll trust and unwaveringly try.

To do all that You ask
And not worry about the task.

If I could give my Life for You

If I could give my life for You the way You gave it to me.
Instead of being absentminded, thoughtless, and full of greed.

If I could die on the cross as You did, Lord
Instead of going through life always and absolutely bored.

If I could get through this season knowing what You did it for.
And not wailing, grieving and always wanting more.

But I can give my life to You, Lord, with one thing in mind.
For You died on that cross for me, and now I'm not blind.

For everything You did, Lord, You did it for all.
And You give us abundant love so that we don't stall.

May we always be ready to share what You did for us.
By helping them to get to know more about You, Jesus.

Now I most humbly and honestly plead,
Give me God's love and not man's greed.

A Cross in you Pocked And an Angel on your Shoulder

With a cross in you pocked and an angel on your shoulder,
It is reminding you that He's beside you and making you bolder.

To guide you and instruct you, to protect and heal you.
To love Him and to pray to Him that's all you have to do.

To know that he died for you, took all your
sins, punishments and cares,
All you have to do is ask for forgiveness and invite Him in if you dare.

The joy and peace that you receive, more that you can believe.
To always be there to help you be all that you can be.

So, this blessing I ask of Him for you, that your
joy be full and your life rich with love,
From your God which is deep inside you and shines from above.

ALL IN ONE

The Father, which does hold together with care
Even the smallest particle of air.

The Holy Spirit, which is the support and will not tare,
He is the power and action beyond compare.

The Son, which is the nucleus of it all,
Because of His crucifixion, salvation He did call.

Put them together in a solitary unit.
You have a power so great nothing can stand up to it.

Though each individually has holy power you can't believe,
Working as a unit it's impossible for the mind to conceive.
He's all in our God. The Holy one of Israel,
We are put here for His pleasure, so understand He is very real.

Are You Prepared

Are you prepared for what He wants of you?
Are you prepared for what He wants you to do?
If not then you'd better pray
That guidance and wisdom within you stay.

Always be on your guard and open in the heart
For you never know just when or how He wants you to start.
We must be prepared to check and to discern
Whether it be from God or not, we must be concerned.

And when we get it just right the miracles do show.
With God's power and might He helps us get up and go.
And still we must be in constant prayer and
stay on guard day and night.
For if we don't stay close to Him we'd be in a terrible plight.

So, we worship, adore and praise Him, thank, seek, and love Him.
For without His guiding light our world would be mighty dim.

FILL MY VESSEL LORD

Fill my vessel, Lord with Your grace
Till there of me is no trace.

Of the worldly person that used to be
And it is only Jesus they see in me.
Fill my vessel, Lord, with your love
So that I know it only comes from above.

That it pours out of my heart in abundance
And in continuous flow, not just once.
Fill my vessel, lord with your overwhelming compassion
So that the things I do are not for an attraction.

But just to please You, Holy Father, and friend,
For You are our God without end.
Fill my vessel, Lord with humbleness of heart,
That I'm always willing to do my part.

That I always know without doubt It's You
That does just what You want me to.

WHEN I LOOK AT A CHRISTMASS TREE

When I look at the decorations on a Christmas tree.
It reminds me of all the wonderful things God gave me.
The topper is an angel, she stands for the
angels God sends around the world.
It's glorious to know that for me those wings unfurl.
Next is the bright and shining lights. They stand for
the cities and towns the world through out.
The different colored light are for the different
races, of their beauty there is no doubt.

The ornaments are for the many blessings He sends our way.
The icicles is the winter wonderland in which we play.
The gifts under the tree are the special love we are to give each one.
The nativity is the reminder that God sent His Son.
The star in the window is a reminder of the Star of David,
That the Jews are His special people, we are to
pray for them and that's God's bid
When we put them all together we know that God sent Jesus His Son,
To save our souls to be with Him eternally. each and every one.

DON'T LOOK FOR TROUBLE

Don't look for trouble looking for a place to happen,
Be ye wise and understanding.
Do not envy or cause strife,
But always seeking Jesus' way of life.
Let us not be self seeking or have selfish ambition,
For every evil thing there is confusion.
For if our motives are right then graciously we act
To those who are against us, we can be for their good and that is a fact.
A servant of the Lord must not quarrel but be genteel to all.
Able to teach, patient, in humility correct those who oppose all.
God will grant them repentance so the will know the truth,
If they come to their senses and escape from
the devil and not remain aloof.
James and Paul are not alone on right
attitudes and motives of the heart.
The bible tells us that if these are not right then we
are of little value for it is a book, a book apart.
And over and over the Word of God calls for the kind
of love that is a motive before it is an action.
So, please don't' be this kind of people, this kind of faction.
For God's love is real for You
Lets make ours for others true.

James 3:13-16, 2 Timothy 2:24-26, 1 Corinthians 13:1-3

A PRAYER FOR A CHILD

Lord, I need Your help with a child I love.
She needs You and Your guidance from above.

She lies, steels, and cheats and goes against her mother's wishes.
I can't get through to her that this too is against Your wishes.

So I put her in Your hands and in Your loving care.
Because I know beyond a shadow of a doubt You will be fair.

That You will do what is right for her
No matter what happens or occurs.

I thank You for that peace
And for that great release.

I give her to Your totally and fee
So that she'll be what You want her to be.

Rest of the Story

Heaven is the rest of the story that's told.
So come boldly to the throne and watch it unfold.

You can't see it or touch it or hold it in your hand.
But it's gloriously clear it is God's perfect plan.

How marvelous it will be when I can behold
The rest of the story that has been told.

The crystal streets all paved with gold,
But mostly to see my friends faces of old.

I Could fill a Book

Oh, Lord, I could fill a book with Your glory and honor and praise,
For all the things You've done for me right up to today, so thanks I say.
The healing strength and improvement and there is so much more.
For there is a definite knowledge that You'll
be there until I reach Your shore.
There are so many blessings, I don't know
about, so many I can't eve guess.
And for these I say Hallelujah, amen and yes.
There is no way to say thank You, although I say it again and again.
For the things You have done for me and for
what You have been, I can't even begin.
So I humbly beg Your pardon for the inadequacy I feel.
And with this problem You too I know will deal.
I love You and appreciate You and try to show You how I care,
By showing people how You care and love me and this love I share.
But it really is so little from this tine speck of dust to do.
Just know and accept this, Lord I really love You too.

His Seasons Approaching

His season's approaching to remind us even more,
Of the blessings and promises He gives us galore.

So, upon Him I praise and do continually thank,
With a promise that you can take to the bank.

That I'll love Him forever and try to do what He tells me.
As He promises I will with Him forever be.

Another Proof

Without His help, nothing would get done.
Even though we think that we could do some.

I look out at the beauty of the yard that was
nothing but brush a short time ago.
And I realize He created all the things there and I know.

I know He is God and no other, I know
the beauty is His and not mine.
I know that the strength He gave me to do it was
His and so is the vine ripe tomatoes on
Which we dine.

The wonderful color of the roses which are so diverse
And the heavenly aroma of the Four O'clocks
matches nothing on earth.

How marvelous to know our God cares even about our senses
That He fills everyone to capacity that passes
and shows that His love is immense.

A Psalm of Praise

O Lord my God, how wonderful You are.
It's so very hard to put into words what You mean to me.

I know Your are close to me, not standing off afar.
I ask only that You guide and direct me and
let me be what You want me to be.
The stars in the heavens are without number just
like the blessings You've given to us.
How can I thank, how can I possibly repay the debt I owe.

For you took all sin, sickness and much, much more without any fuss.
And with mercy, kindness, understanding and
great love upon us you do bestow.

HOPE OF GLORY

You are the hope of Glory,
I will be glad to tell Your story.

I want them to know of Your mercy, and grace.
I want them to see Your glorious face.

I want to have You so deep inside of me.
That it isn't me but You they see.

I will study and rightly divide Your Word.
And in Your armor myself I will gird.

I want to be so full of the joy of You,
That they ask how they can have that too.

I want to be able to speak of You with boldness,
Drawing more people unto You in righteousness.

All this and more I am receiving
Because of Your glory and grace I'm believing.

INSURMOUNTABLE MOUNTAINS

The mountain I'm crossing seems insurmountable,
The crossing of which looks impossible.

After I cross that one, there's one even higher.
My will gets less and my strength is getting weaker.

My time is running out and I'm on my last hope.
Isn't there somebody out there that can help me cope?

Then someone told me of a Savior so great
That He takes all my troubles and a new live in me He creates.

All the while I was struggling He was right by my side.
All I had to do was give Him my pride.

Believe in who He said He was
And get others to believe in His cause.

I do this gladly with deep gratitude and love.
Because He's the Son of God come down from above.

Deny Him Never

I'm predestined to be adopted by a perfect God Father.
He knows the beginning to the end of the mater.

He knows my choices before I make them.
Yet, he gave me free will to choose him.

He knows indeed, whether I'm good or bad.
He even knows if I'm happy or sad.

How awesome our loving God is
And to know that we are ever His.

I will sing His praises and glory forever.
And I pray I'll deny Him never.

A Gift for Jesus

What gift did you bring to Jesus for His birthday today?
Do you know the meaning of Christmas and all that it portrays?

The special gift that you should give to Jesus
is to love Him, trust and obey.
For what greater gift could you give to Jesus that this, today.

For in remembering His birth you should also remember His dying.
Also, the fact that He promised a second coming.

Without these facts the birth is like any other,
There would have been no point for Him to bother.

So, remember all that Jesus is,
By accepting that we are well and truly His.

SING WITH THE ANGELS

We are on the way to see all He has for us.
Because in Jesus we've put our trust.

He's told us how it would be,
We just have to read the Bible and see.

How before the throne we sing praise to His name
And they'll be no worry of riches or fame.

We'll be walking on streets of gold
And visit with the prophets of old.

Oh what a glorious time will be had.
There will be no time to be miserable or sad.

I just can't wait for Him to come and get me.
I'll be singing with the angels. How happy I'll be.

My Prayer for God's Children

It's easy to see and condemn others actions
while being blinded by our own.
So I pray that the Holy Spirit that indwells will show
the seeds of wickedness we have sown.

That we might repent and ask forgiveness,
And be prepared to live in righteousness.

That we constantly and with compassion
draw as many as we can to Him.
It won't pay the debt but it will glorify Him within.

Then all who see us will be in no doubt.
That we are His Children, will be even beyond the very end.

II Samuel 12:5
And David's anger greatly kindled against the man;
And said to Nathan, as the Lord liveth, the man
that hath done this thing shall surely die.

SELF SEEKING

I pray, Father God, don't let me be self seeking.
Always after the world trekking.
And when the deed I do in Your name,
Please let be from my heart, not bring You shame.

Let the words I profess be honest and true.
Show in wisdom that could only come from You.
Let the grace and love that springs from my heart,
Show only that for You I'm doing my part.

Let me always be willing to share
The Gospel, our Word, with loving care.
Let my life show forth to end,
That Jesus is my Savior, Brother, God, friend.

Let the world see that they too can have this same peace
By believing, repenting, and forgiveness of
sin, then to Him themselves release.

REMEMBER

I was born on this day with a great task before me.
To do what the Father asked and to be what He wanted me to be.

I was born in a lowly manger,
And to most I would, stay a stranger.

I would die a young man but not in vain.
Because I would rise and come again.

That was my great commission.
To give my life for the sin of the world and I did in completion.

So when you think of my birthday at this time of year,
Remember the rest of my life and make it clear

To the rest of that is steeped in sin,
The passage John 3:16 and what is written within.

SHOW FORTH HIS ATTRIBUTES

Attributes we don't delve into much.
But, Jesus' are so real you can reach out and touch.

If we study His life so rich and full,
He draws us in with a compelling pull.

So loving and giving, there has never been
Anyone like Him now or then.

No greater love has any man but he lay down His life for a friend.
He did this for me and you that we might follow His trend.

That we might love one another with such great joy
And realize He is not just a story nor a toy.

THE PROOF

He us the Word but so much more.
You can't count the blessings He has in store.

Obedience is all He asks of you,
Just by walking in Jesus' shoes.

It sounds impossible but really it's not,
That's the very reason with Satan He fought.

The fight He has already won
For each and every blessed one.

It is hard to define one who is indefinable,
Just remember that no matter what He is unchangeable.

So remember THE WORD is the Life and truth.
Just believe in Him and you'll fine the proof.

FRIEND

When I go to heaven I'll never go hungry or thirsty.
Although on earth I've been both.

Jesus fill to overflowing and life giving eternity.
If the world sees you in trouble the just stand aloof.

But to know that my God is our eternal hope
Is a blessing beyond anything I can comprehend.

He gives me everything I need to cope,
And gives me all the time with Him I need to spend.

Can you imagine a better friend
Than one who is there when or wherever you call.

One who is with you to the very end
And one who lift you when you fall.

Better than this He has provided for me a home.
Better than anything here on earth.

On this planed I could search and comb,
And not finding anything so great. He planned it from my very birth.

BREATH OF GOD

The very breath of God is our Holy Spirit
And that He lives in us, well, I can hardly believe it.

The awesome knowledge that He breaths in us
Is beyond understanding but it's where I put my trust.

To know that ever breath I take and every thought I have
Leads me down His ever guiding path.

Always urging, sympathizing and
Willing to lend a helping hand.

So the next time you take a breath, remember you share it with His.
And watch where that breath takes you as you remember this.

OFFENDED FRIEND

I have offended thee friend
And I will bear the burden to the end.
I know in my heart that it surely was not my intention.
The insight was not my invention.

I have prayed deep and hard asking from where it came.
The answer is always the ever the same.
While the message was chosen to be delivered by me,
God only knows, I didn't want it to be.

Then after it blew up in my face
And of the friendship there was not left a trace,
Doubts would come and Satan would be there
Hounding me telling me, "Why should you care?"

But You are a gentle person God
And I know in His pathway you do walk,
And why He gave me the message He did I do not know.
The Lord has chosen this on me to bestow.

But always and ever you'll be in my prayers
And though you may not believe it I really do care.
And though you may not again call me friend,
In my mind and heart I'll still be yours to the end.

It's not Enough

Knowledge is not enough, you must truly believe.
Only then of His gifts can you receive.

It's not enough to just read His Word, you must put it into practice.
It's not enough to say you love man, you must
let it pour out of your soul for us.

It's not enough to ask Jesus to take care of your troubles,
You must then turn them over to Him, leave
your hands off, knowing He is able.

It's not enough to say you'll pray for someone
you must find a closed and climb in.
It's not enough to die for Christ, you must be willing to live for Him.

THE PROCLESS GIFT

Each year at this time, I try to reflect
His grace and love that I respect.
Because the priceless gift He gave
For us our lives and souls to save.

He sent His Son in man's own form,
To save their souls as He has sworn.
His love, grace and mercy is beyond measure,
A gift to go beyond earthly treasure.

So when I look upon all the gifts
The one I don't see is the one my heart, it lifts.
To know that He gave such a gift so priceless,
That I can do nothing else but accept His righteousness.

GOD'S GIFT

You are God's gift to us,
You serve us with no fuss.
The work that you do
Is dedicated and true.
You work night and day,
And in God you do stay.
To teach us and guide us
Abut the man called Jesus.
About the life He led
And you make sure we are fed
With God's true word of life
And with His power ease our strife.
So we say to you too
This poem was written for you
On this Joyous Christ's season.
With great though and reason.
You are God's gift to us, that we may behold
The Christ child's life unfurled unfold.
We are returning your gift of love and sharing
With our gift of your love and caring.
May the Joy of the Lord be with you.
And may God bless you.

TREASURE

If everything I have, time, talents, treasures, is God's
Then I should be pretty grateful the He allows me to use it.
To be consciously aware of each one He allots,
And to be very careful not to abuse it.
I want to be committed to all He has given
To share and care for what He has commissioned.
To show them how their life is worth liven
When washed in the blood for the sins for remission.

To show that the treasures I've collected through the years
Have been Your blessing given by Your grace.
It is not gold, jewels or material things that are so dear.
Just peace, love and joy, of woe there is not a trace.

These wonderful treasures God gave to me
Doing what He asked of me with a whole heart.
All I had to do was get down on my knees
Receive and love Him that's how to start.

The Stranger in the Mirror

When I looked into the mirror.
I saw an old woman. I wondered who she
as. She looked a little familiar.
But the gray and the wrinkles threw me
because I don't remember seeing her.

She seems nice enough, am I seeing the real her?
Then with insight and a strange beat of my heart,
I knew her, my spirit gave a stir.
It was like looking back through the eyes of a stranger.
Gone is the hardness and selfishness
And in it's place, what an exposure.
A little wisdom and peace, tolerance and compassion.
The woman looking back at me is so
Different in comparison.
I like this one better but still she could grow.
With the help of the Lord, slow the old self does go.

THE FORGIVENESS THING

Asking forgiveness is hard to do.
Giving it is even harder too.

Jesus did it for everyone here
And requests that in us it does appear.

We must ask Him to put it into our hearts
So that there is not and inkling or part

That is not filled with this forgiveness thing.
So that we can be just like Jesus in our very being.

For when we do this, love and compassion follows through,
Then in turn it makes forgiveness easier to do.

RESTING IN GOD

Testing in God is an honest wisdom of the heart,
Which when we have it nothing can tear us apart.

When we allow the peace of God to rest upon us
Our lives don't have minuses, just one big plus.

When His wisdom to daily live within
There's nothing we can' face, nothing we can't win.

When trouble is around us and we laugh our fears away,
You can be your resting in God, your enemies He does slay.

When in the deepest gloom the rainbow does shine,
You know you can dig down in the snow and the rose you shall find.
Resting in God is and honest wisdom of the heart,
What a beautiful way for the day to start.

James 3:17,18
But the wisdom that is from above is first pure, then
peaceable, gentle, and easy to be entreated, full of
mercy and good fruits, without partiality.
And without hypocrisy. And the fruit of righteousness
is sown in peace of them that make peace.

A GIFT OF GOD

On Christmas day a babe was born,
And because of this my life was torn,

Between the world and His grace.
The choice was easy when I saw His face.

I think of how He walked through life,
Bearing loneliness, heartbreak, suffering and strife.

Through all this the gifts He gave,
His love, His healing, and the souls He saved.

So, with His suffering and His shame,
The true meaning of Christmas to me came.

Like the star that shown divine
I'll do my best to let His light shine.

CHRIST CHILD

I was holding a child as I sat by the Christmas tree,
Singing Christmas Carols and feeling carefree.

Then I imagined what it would have been like back then.
Back in the stable where it all began.

To hear the angels sing and the star shine above,
Knowing that what He brought the world was love.

There is no greater gift, and for this His life He gave.
He loves us so much that our lives He saved.

When I came back to earth I had tears in my eyes.
Tears of joy and happiness and love, I cried.

So, remember the Christ child born upon this day,
Fill you heart with His love and try hard to give it away.

I Had walked life's Way

I had walked life's way with an easy tread,
Had followed where comforts and pleasures led.
Until one day in a quiet place,
I met the Master face to face.
With station and rank and wealth for my goal,
Much thought for my body, but not my soul.
I met Him and knew Him and I blushed to see,
That His eyes full of sorrow were fixed on me.
And I faltered and fell at His feet that day,
While my castles and wealth melted away.
Melted and vanished and in their place,
Naught else could I see but my Masters face.
And I cried aloud, o make me meek,
To follow the steps of Thy wounded feet.
My thought is now for the souls of men;
I've lost my life to find it again.
Ever since that day in a quiet place,
I met my Master face to face.

Enough

He gives us enough grace for change,
To guide our lives and rearrange.

To make us in to Hi glorious likeness,
And an example of His perfectness.

To show all the world what He can do
With the power of His grace and love through me and you.

Show how He can turn a sinful man
Into all that He had for us planed.

Showing kindness and love to all who accept,
But for others He's surely wept.

Let us do all that we can
To show the world we've made our stand.

CHILDREN

We thank you, children, for the joy you bring into our lives.
To make you into responsible beautiful adults
is that thing for which we strive.
The love you give so spontaneously and freely
Enriches our lives so much we can't put it in words easily.

The hope of us doing the same can only be done through Christ Jesus.
We pray for Him to guide and protect you
and ask that you do also for us.
Together we'll walk the path He has for us chosen
And through Him we'll know which way we are going.

Remember when sometimes we speak in anger or frustration
It's not because we love you less only that
we wish to correct your action.

That love we have for you is deep and abiding,
Even though sometimes it's a little in hiding.
We love you and we would eve go so far as to down our lives lay.
Just as Jesus our love for you will be always.

TIME

I remember when now was in the distant
future. How hast time rushed by.
It should serve to us a reminder that the time
for drawing souls to God is nigh.

If time was running short them
It must be down to the last second now.

So help me Lord, so and be better than I've ever been.
That I might be a leader showing where, when and how.

When my dear Savior and Lord does come,
I won't be found wanting by His majesty.

I want nothing more than His well done
And to show Him my love for Him fills me deeply.

Printed in the United States
By Bookmasters